LAST POEMS

———

Roy McFadden

edited by
Sarah Ferris

Abbey Press

First published in November 2002 in an edition of 1,000 copies

Abbey Press
Newry Office
Courtenay Hill, Newry, County Down
Northern Ireland, BT34 2ED

A CIP record for this book is available from the British Library

ISBN: 1 901617 21 1
Author: McFadden, Roy
Title: Last Poems
Format: 138 mm x 214 mm
2002

Design: Adrian Rice
Frontispiece by Rowel Friers
Typesetting by David Anderson in 11/14.5pt Sabon
Printed by Nicholson & Bass Ltd, Belfast

CONTENTS

Acknowledgments

The editor would like to acknowledge Margaret McFadden for generously giving permission to publish *Last Poems*, and Yvonne Friers for permission to reproduce Rowel B. Friers' etching of Roy McFadden as a frontispiece for this book. Thanks are also due to Philip Hobsbaum for his help and encouragement, and to Adrian Rice and Abbey Press for making this publication possible.

Abbey Press would also like to acknowledge the support of their patrons: Seamus Heaney, Gerard Trainor and Padraig and Nicky McGuinness.

Editor's Note

What can we say, here, by the hardening fire,
As the clock ticks history, and the flowers drip blood?

Roy McFadden, 'Poem for Today', 1943

Roy McFadden died on September 15, 1999. I met him four years earlier through my research on John Hewitt. He was a generous and patient mentor who increasingly entrusted me with his manuscripts and papers. During his final illness, he gave me this last set of nineteen poems. Overwhelmingly elegiac in tone, these have been kept as he ordered them. From our conversations, Roy McFadden would have been delighted with this publication. It comprises a moving requiem for a craftsman of elegance and integrity, who was burdened by a duty to 'capture and immobilise / The transient moments' ('Granny Bell') and small sufferings of his country's 'congregation of stopped mouths' ('Replaying Old Gramaphone Records'). Remembering this, I commend these poems to those who, in his words, "prefer to read, rather than be read at".

Sarah Ferris
Autumn 2002

Introduction

Roy McFadden in his lifetime presented the aspect of a Belfast solicitor, which is what he was. On closer acquaintance, one noticed the massive brow enhanced by its baldness, the shrewd but guarded glance, and the voice precise in language as in articulation. All this suggested that here was no ordinary lawyer.

As well as serving the law for almost sixty years, Roy McFadden was one of the most distinguished writers in a Northern Irish constellation that included John Hewitt, Robert Greacen, W.R. Rodgers, Sam Hanna Bell and Joseph Tomelty. McFadden's first major publication was *Swords and Ploughshares* (1943), published by Routledge at the instigation of Herbert Read, whose political anarchism he shared. It showed the influence of Yeats, as did his subsequent collections of 1945 and 1947 respectively. Indeed, the development of McFadden's writing could be summarised as an effort to come to terms with the older poet.

After *The Heart's Townland* (1947), McFadden published no major collection for twenty-four years. In the interim, he developed his legal practice, and helped to raise his five children – he had married Margaret Ferguson in 1952. He still found time to start a literary magazine, *Lagan*, in 1945 and to co-edit another, *Rann*, which flourished from 1948 to 1953. Later, his acidic tones became well known on radio, presenting from 1949 until 1963 a regular programme, *The Arts in Ulster*, in collaboration with his life-long friend, the playwright and producer John Boyd.

The bitter circumstances of Northern Ireland decreed that McFadden develop as a war poet. A human voice emerged from what had been Yeatsian rhetoric. *The Garryowen* (1971) possesses an unforced authority, while *A Watching Brief* (1978) benefits from the fact that McFadden had a defined job, that of a lawyer going through the forms and ceremonies of a precariously law-abiding city.

Roy McFadden was one of that rare band of poets whose writing improved with the years. A late volume, *After*

Seymour's Funeral (1990), is probably his finest, showing, as Edna Longley wrote, "a fastidious clarity of feeling". The Yeats' practice, summoning up contemporaries from the dead, is here fully absorbed into McFadden's characteristic style. The title poem, which may prove to be one of his best remembered, evokes friends whom he has seen grow old, people whose wills he has made, those whose funerals he has attended.

A *Collected Poems* was published by Lagan Press, Belfast, in 1996. It includes many poems and translations that McFadden had previously chosen not to publish. It also incorporates a collection subsequent to *Seymour* and not issued separately: *The Hunger Marchers: Poems 1990–1995*. Of the poems there, 'The Low Glen', 'Miss Purdy in Old Age', 'Miss Walters' and 'Prior Title' will bear especial attention –

> Bow Street and Market Square. Belfast
> On Fridays? Did he daily check his watch
> Against the townhall clock? On market days
> Hide typists from the farmers? ...
> ... Did he
> Watch hard men blubber over grudging wills?
> ('Prior Title')

This, of a solicitor who died nine years before the author was born.

This sense of continuity with times past marks the present collection, McFadden's final contribution to the world of letters. It is poetry in all senses of recollection – the production, as one might expect, of an old man. But that is the same as saying the posthumously published *Last Poems* of another fine poet, D. H. Lawrence, is the writing of a sick man. What matters is not whether the writer is old or sick but what he does with such circumstances.

In *Last Poems*, McFadden is very likely the only person who still remembers 'Granny Bell' –

> She'd watch the Green from her dark porch
> While children played, like branches strummed by a
> breeze.

In 'Animal Shelter, May Street' the present shelter merges with the memory of one long past –

> You recall
> That other dog's lament
> In the deserted house and your
> Need to return to share his fear and grief,
> …

One of the best poems here, 'Twilight in Joy Street', achieves an elegiacally characteristic dying fall in remembering a shy girl hurrying through the gathering mist –

> When twilight sighed and closed on her quick step
> Fading and fraying into indifferent night.

There are contemporaries in age tidying up the remnants of their lives, in 'Bonfire' –

> He'd burned the lot, he said:
> Poems and drawings, journals, catalogues

And in 'Late Visit to a Friend' –

> Saint Francis for an August afternoon
> He ministers to the birds,
> At times including to attend
> The silence brushing past our parrying words.

As in 'After Seymour's Funeral', McFadden sees himself as the recorder of past events in 'Hospital Blue' –

> The faded uniforms and faces stay
> Imprinted on a scene
> Entrusted, say, to my safekeeping now.

And in 'Girl with a String of Beads' –

> What happened to that afternoon,
> I said rather than asked.

What happened to it? It is right here, recollected in this poem –

> … that afternoon in the photograph,
> In the garden, when I suppose
> She was 9 or 10 years old, allowed
> To pose with her mother's beads; but with a smile
> All hers alone as she returned
> The watching camera's calculating stare.

These elegant recollections ratify the claim made at the end of 'After Seymour's Funeral': "Now only I remember …". In these poems McFadden appears as unimpeachable witness; seldom as an actor. Yet in the richness of his memories a sense of life stirs when facile headlines – even topical poems – have faded and been forgotten.

These poems – and this is true of McFadden's sixty years of output – do not yield all their meaning to the casual or superficial glance. The discerning reader will find a shrewd, though guarded survey of experience, an articulation precise as to observation and language. The term 'presences' is a key one in his poems, first and last:

> Such visitations, guidances,
> As signalled to the poet William Yeats
> When he willed presences
> To occupy and dominate the room?
> ('Replaying Old Gramophone Records')

Or again, from 'Portrait of a Poet' written a half century earlier –

> He culled as it were from the air
> Not their ghosts but their smiling presences
> Inhabiting gardens and strict avenues:

Philip Hobsbaum

GRANNY BELL

On sunburnt August afternoons,
Fuchsias inert, the rowans ruminant,
She'd watch the Green from her dark porch
While children played, like branches strummed by a breeze.

Given the words, she might have said
She was an open window, through which trees
Cajoled and idle clouds inquired;
Or else, closing her eyes, spun out a spell

To capture and immobilise
The transient moments, lithe like a held branch,
Girls' laughter, ducklings braving the stream,
The church with its fidgeting pews, rustles and coughs:

Then, holding her breath, marvelled to find
That she was able somehow to contain
Those fading momentary truths
Intact in a silence lapping remembering shores.

(3 June 1996)

ANIMAL SHELTER, MAY STREET

Times, distances, converge
In side-streets silted up
With shadows; silhouettes
Menace, seduce, command.
But in the empty thoroughfare,
Frigid under the lights, a threat's
Only the echo of your heels,
Challenging silence, measuring absences,
Daring the ambush crouched behind the wall.

A dog howls in the dark,
Beyond the frigid street's
Starched silence. You recall
That other dog's lament
In the deserted house and your
Need to return to share his fear and grief,
Making his cry your own
In your own emptiness.

And now in the empty street
You face a later, skid-marked thoroughfare,
That dead dog in your arms, staining your coat;
And stand aside to join
Gathering silences,
Shadows of voices silting up your heart.

(12 June 1996)

TWILIGHT IN JOY STREET

Twilights were never sinister,
Hostile, malevolent,
When safe in the loitering light
Expectant destinations opened arms
To homecomings along untroubled streets.

Then, outside open doors at noon,
Upright on kitchen chairs,
Old men dreamed in the sun;
And later, indoors, bent to the vesper-bell,
Evening's caress, matching the street-lamp's glow.

Before you glimpsed the kerchiefed head
Shaking off gathering mist,
You sensed her hurrying step,
Her small voice hanging back from a hallo,
The glance downcast but half-acknowledging;

Then lost her to the emptying town,
On past the pub's red eye,
Sisters-of-Mercy's school,
When twilight sighed and closed on her quick step
Fading and fraying into indifferent night.

(18 July 1996)

BONFIRE

He'd burned the lot, he said:
Poems and drawings, journals, catalogues
Of exhibitions (Middleton and Luke,
Conor and Nietsche); programmes from the Group;
Bundles of letters kept
From years before the war –
Incinerated in an afternoon.

Discouraging reproach,
A late springclean, a redding-up, he said.
But one suspected it was more than that.
An imperfection in his work, a lack
Of vision in his art,
Might have seemed heresies
To be eliminated in the fire.

Once in a while, in chat,
He'd talk about 'the end' derisively.
Purged now, perhaps, with brushes set aside
And pens and pencils on the mantelshelf,
He's free to challenge life
Without the need to tell
Or hang another picture on the wall.

(31 August 1996)

HOSPITAL BLUE

Along the Cairnburn Road
On warm midsummer days,
They'd sit on banks, lean awkwardly on walls,
And silently converse
Abstractedly with old remembering trees.

Blue uniforms informed
On their identity:
Discarded wrecks sent home from the Great War,
Shellshocked, distraught, aghast,
To cultivate the silences of trees.

Occasional trees survive;
And in their silences
The faded uniforms and faces stay
Imprinted on a scene
Entrusted, say, to my safekeeping now.

(11 September 1996)

THE LIG

Midsummer evening, still
Tepid with sunshine, redolent
Of new-mown grass in gardens; trees
Catching their breath back from the languid air:

When, raucously, a voice
Rounded the corner with its song;
The singer then, in cast-off clothes,
Dressed as a girl, striking an attitude:

Stockings in holes, a shawl
Crooked across the pinned-up dress,
A cloche hat crushed over the brow;
The song a maudlin favourite of the day.

He sang expansively,
Brushing the mimicry aside:
Not just for pennies, when, at heart,
He serenaded balconies for love.

Later, after he'd gone,
Evening composed itself; the trees
Preened leaves; and pale piano notes
Tiptoed across correct conforming lawns.

(16 November 1996)

WICKET-KEEPING: SCHOOL XI

Laconic overhead,
Scrabo Tower like an umpire's finger raised
In judgment; but, beyond,
Approaching the outfield
Summer, footloose like a girl then you'd have said,
Carrying flowers, with sunshine in her hair.

Resilient, grass-stem-sweet,
Turf buoyed you up, cushioned your scrambling sprawl,
Cajoled the swerving ball
Into expectant gloves;
And (yes) tholed bold incursive buttercups
Like picnickers inside the boundary line.

White-padded, yellow-gloved,
Guardian, despoiler, close conspirator
You read the bowler's arm
For spin; further afield,
Glanced once again before you recognised
Classmates apotheosised by the game.

And, changing ends, remarked
For reappraisal, now, in retrospect,
Wise after the event,
On your duality,
Watcher, participant; and noted too
The unremitting judgment on the hill.

(19 February 1997)

JESSIE MATTHEWS

Singer and dancer, once a star,
Eclipsed for a decade, she came
Out of retirement to perform
In drama, only for the pit
To shout its preference for a song,
A maudlin call for some old souvenir.

Taking her bow without a smile,
Miss Jessie Matthews coldly said
She'd never set her foot again
Upon a Belfast stage; declared
That her first visit to their town
Would also – a closed gesture – be her last.

But, Jessie Matthews, let me say
Across the years that I for one,
Dumbfounded in that rowdy hall,
Recalled the way your radiance
Illuminated lives, your voice
Caressed each vowel, clasped each consonant.

(11 May 1957)

THE WELSH MATCH

The red trams, open-ended at the top,
    Hirpled and clanged and rang;
2d, they said, would get you anywhere.
Street-lamps, knocked up at dusk, coughed, said ahem;
    Later, crooned lullabies.

In those days we played Wales at Ravenhill.
    Saturday-morning's streets
Made way for scarves and favours, red and white
Insignia; gesticulating trams
    Stormed, swaggered to the ground.

The games themselves were rarely memorable;
    The chant alone remains.
But I recall small children frenziedly
Scrambling for pennies tossed down from the trams
    On threadbare thoroughfares.

(21 April 1997)

REPLAYING OLD GRAMOPHONE RECORDS

Life moves to free
From a guarded gathered silence
All those stilled voices shut away
In darkness, a congregation of stopped mouths,
When stylus and record meet,
Like the press of a switch amazing a room with light:

Restored to sound,
Not just for another hearing,
Belated encore, a replay,
Or for the welling of a weeping wound,
A sharp nostalgic cry,
But for time itself checking its stride to hear.

Should you confront
An ultimate, posthumous silence,
What, if a seam loosened and broke
To free a voice, might mumble back to sound:
Repeat performances?
Or those same accents in a different play?

How would you greet
From an unravelling silence
Such visitations, guidances,
As signalled to the poet William Yeats
When he willed presences
To occupy and dominate the room?

(21 June 1997)

THE ROYAL BOX

Scots comics hailed us from the stage –
'The rich folk have arrived' – with mock
Respect to make the gods and groundlings laugh.
Beside my modest competence
My two companions, newly-rich,
Smiled down as if acknowledging applause:

While, out of place and character,
Outsider lacking party card,
Exposed to stage and auditorium,
The nudging joke, the belly-laugh,
I turned away; but afterwards
Raked back the ashes, looking for a sign:

And found an older memory,
A pantomime on Christmas Eve
Where as a child I turned from masquerade
Back home to actualities,
Holly festooned round picture frames,
Shining like childhood till it wilted too.

(5 July 1997)

THE FLOWERSELLERS AT THE CITY HALL

Rainswept flagstones framed and mirrored back
Bouquets and sprays like a still life,
A pavement-artist's *oeuvre;*
While, shawled and buttoned from the rain,
Conor-like figures stood addressing life.

'She'd buy a rose', you said, 'a single rose' –
Recalling childhood's treats downtown –
'Caress her cheek with it,
Then lay it gently on my palm;
A kind of benediction it seems now'.

My grandmother as well, although estranged
From *my* childhood, mythologised
To a blurred image now
Of someone in a rainy street,
Holding a rose out to a laughing girl.

(26 July 1997)

CHURCH ORGANIST

Accosted in the street
Or answering the phone,
With tongue in cheek he'd try to disconcert –
'I haven't seen you for an age' –
Scolding a voice he thought he recognised.

Securing a chair, he'd splay
Out fingers to explore
The grain, the crafted style of arm and leg,
Degree of workmanship;
While all the while engaging you in chat.

And, travelling on his own
Down town on bus or tram,
He'd know the stop, and how to find his way
To organ-practice in the church,
Like Raftery to play to empty pews.

At harvest festivals,
Close in his dark alcove,
Inhaling scents denied appearances,
He'd flex his fingers to recall
From thwarted vision certainty of sound.

(28 October 1997)

LATE VISIT TO A FRIEND

He scatters nuts for the birds
Buoyant under the leaves,
While petulant hens scrabble and scrape;
And, nudged by a sauntering breeze,
Lifts up his head to reminisce,
As though inspired by the decades ringing in the trees.

'I'm happy enough', he says,
Seemingly reconciled,
Leaning against an acquiescent tree.
Too soon clerics will corner him
And usher up his thoughts to God
And the shining acres of the Promised Land.

I was here when he planted the trees,
Built the stout house beyond;
Shared hooleys that harried the fields
With a frenzy of fiddles and songs
Hushed only by the scrake of dawn,
Turf dead on the hearth and the candles with blackened tongues.

The ruminating breeze
Shoulders up close to him.
Saint Francis for an August afternoon
He ministers to the birds,
At times inclining to attend
The silence brushing past our parrying words.

(20 August 1998)

DISTANT RELATIONS

– Now and again, McKelvey said,
At weddings, funerals,
Approaching faces smile and say
Vaguely familiar names,
Some prefixed *Judge,* or even *Sir;*
And you recall
A junior counsel briefed occasionally
For minor court appearances,
Or else a client you advised
For some small fee or without fee at all:
And look again
For a connection between then and now.

Alert to cross the street, he said,
To shun establishment,
Collusion with authority,
You lose the ready smile,
The easy greeting, the trite words;
Then, face to face,
No street to cross, no corner to turn round,
But cornered in a room,
You summon back assuaging words
To cover up the wounds of difference,
Admonished by
The gathering silence that confronts us all.

(6 July 1998)

STORMONT 1927

The rampant flames implied
Crackle and spit of whin,
And turned the green hillside
Orange against the sky.

They were clearing the ground, he said,
For an Ulster parliament,
To keep watch overhead
On six disjointed fields.

A protestant parliament for
A protestant people, he said:
Easy, if unaware
Of prophecy in the flames.

(20 July 1998)

THE 100-FRANC GESTURE

At a café in Saint Germain the other night –
Wet lights like laughter hiccuping down the street –
A young man, putty-faced, with cherub's curls,
Peddled his manuscripts from beer to beer.
Stranger in the city, I thought it right
To buy a poem for five hundred francs;
You'd pay as much for a trite souvenir.

But my companion, a shrewd connoisseur
Of fakes, pretensions and effronteries,
Said no, the verse was bad, and he knew better
Thirsty poets; so one hundred francs
Would be correct. So as I'd give a penny
To some smudged pavement artist, I conferred
My token charity, and didn't buy.

But now I know I should have bought the poem,
Good, bad, or just indifferent toothpaste verse:
For, look, the knowing world fobs off the poet,
Friendly enough but firmly uncommitted,
With such a gesture worth one hundred francs;
Or pays the price, to leave the manuscript
Beside the ashtray and the empty glass.

(Revised 8 August 1998)

LAST VISIT

'You have left your mark', I said,
Holding his dying hands.
Half-sigh, half-smile, and then:
'Not very deep', he said, sideways to God.

Irrelevant in the end,
Targets, achievements, fame,
Remembrances even, fade
From thoughts intent on clutching fickle breath.

Downstairs, directionless
Among the furniture,
Pushing past vacant chairs,
The big dogs ponder, probing his not being there.

And under indifferent trees
Birds have stopped foraging
For nuts from his scattering hand,
Held in mine now, and faltering towards goodbye.

(January 1999)

GIRL WITH A STRING OF BEADS

What happened to that afternoon,
I said rather than asked.
She fingered her throat, looking away,
Back I supposed to a blurred hinterland
Of Kirkwood's Farm, McConnell's Field,
And the idle road ambling between the towns:

To that afternoon in the photograph,
In the garden, when I suppose
She was 9 or 10 years old, allowed
To pose with her mother's beads; but with a smile
All hers alone as she returned
The watching camera's calculating stare.

(18 March 1999)

She, whom I met among sore graves and when
My words were floral tributes, my steps were
Cut by curt death: I could not welcome her
Although I needed her as nine needs ten.

But she accepted while the friends dropped off.
While they equated poet with the grave,
She saw a man to love, a father's face
Would favour five fair children. Those who have targets
Are enemies of love.

Without her I would be an onlooker,
Closing the door and tidying the room,
Shining mirror's verse and prose;
Wiping the terse message on the tomb
Polished granite lengthening the scar
The private album closing the lost war.